ZION
WILLIAMSON

THE ROAD TO
NEW ORLEANS

GIL CONRAD

Zion Williamson: The Road to New Orleans

Full Tilt Press
42964 Osgood Road
Fremont, CA 94539
readfulltilt.com

Full Tilt Press publications may be purchased for educational, business, or sales promotional use.

Design and layout by Sara Radka

Image Credits
AP Images: Icon Sportswire/Jaylynn Nash, cover, 1; Getty Images: Grant Halverson, 14, groveb,
background, Kevin C. Cox, 16, Matrosovv, 4 (silhouette), Mike Coppola, 7, Patrick Smith, 19, 24,
Sarah Stier, 27, Streeter Lecka, 8, 20; Newscom: Cal Sport Media/Jacob Kupferman, 4 (Zion),
Icon Sportswire/Brian Rothmuller, 12, MEGA/AFF-USA.com/O'Connor, 11, TNS/Raleigh News &
Observer/Robert Willett, 23, TNS/The Slate/Tracy Glantz, 18; Pixabay: OpenClipart-Vectors, 5, 30

ISBN: 978-1-62920-832-9 (library binding)
ISBN: 978-1-62920-833-6 (paperback)
ISBN: 978-1-62920-834-3 (ePUB eBook)

CONTENTS

ZION

The University of Virginia's De'Andre Hunter catches a pass on the **baseline**. De'Andre is wide open. He launches a three-point shot. Meanwhile, Duke's Zion Williamson is tracking from the other end of the court. In a flash, the 18-year-old freshman takes off. Less than two seconds later, Zion has run 25 feet! He leaps high into the air and swats Hunter's shot. It goes deep into the stands. Amazement floods through the building. Fans, coaches, and players look up at the replay. Are their eyes playing tricks on them? *Did he really do that?!*

----

baseline: the line on a basketball court that is located behind the backboard at either end of the court

Zion Williamson is an incredible natural athlete. He stands 6 feet, 7 inches tall. He weighs 285 pounds. But even with all that muscle and height, he moves like lightning. His size, speed, and athleticism are perfect for basketball. Zion dunks from high above the rim. He has a smooth **jumper**. And he can dribble and pass like a guard. Wherever Zion has played, he has seen great success. His big smile has led him to become a favorite of teammates, coaches, and fans.

Zion grew up in South Carolina. His physical talent helped him become an incredible high school basketball player. No one was surprised when he earned a **scholarship** to Duke University. After just one year in college, it was clear that Zion was destined for NBA greatness. His season at Duke was a success. It led him to being the number-one pick in the 2019 NBA **draft**.

The best is yet to come for Zion. "I'll do whatever I need to do to win," he said. As bright as his future looks, one thing is for sure: watching him will be a delight for fans. His career with the New Orleans Pelicans will be filled with high-flying dunks and jaw-dropping blocks. Zion is a player no basketball fan will want to miss.

----

jumper: an attempt to score a basket by jumping straight up in the air and shooting the ball while in the air

scholarship: money given to a student by a university to help pay for their education

draft: a system where sports teams choose players from high school or college

Zion Williamson at the 2019 NBA Draft

CHAPTER 2

Zion soars through the air for a dunk against the Syracuse Orange.

GROWING UP

Zion grew up in Florence, South Carolina. Its population is less than 40,000. Even at five years old, Zion knew exactly what he wanted to do. He wanted to be a basketball player. He even told his stepfather, Lee Anderson, that he was going to play in the NBA one day. Instead of laughing, Anderson took young Zion seriously. Anderson worked him hard. He signed Zion up with the Sumter Falcons, a local basketball team. Zion was just five years old. The team was filled with nine-year-olds. But Zion was athletic. He was willing to work. The kindergartner became one of the best players on the team. Zion would wake up at five o'clock every morning to run drills and practice with his stepdad.

Starting when he was seven years old, Zion went to the outdoor courts at McLeod Park to practice. This was something he did most mornings—even before school. The skills he perfected during those early morning workouts would one day make him a legend.

His passion for hoops continued. By the time Zion reached middle school, it was obvious that he had real talent. But the coach of his middle school team was tough. Sharonda Sampson was extra hard on him. She pushed Zion to take extra shots after practice. Every day, she made sure Zion was giving his best effort. Zion later called her "the toughest coach" he had ever played for. But Sampson has a special relationship with Zion, and extra reason to push him to do his best. She is his mother! Zion did an interview just after being selected as the number-one pick in the NBA draft. He made sure that "Coach Mom" got the credit she deserved. "I wouldn't be here without my mom," he said, tears running down his face. "She did everything for me. She put her dreams aside for mine."

Lee Anderson, Zion Williamson, Sharonda Sampson, and Noah Anderson attended the ESPY Awards in 2019. There, Zion won the award for Best College Athlete.

CHAPTER 3

Zion Williamson attended the Adidas Nations Global championship in 2016, where he finished in the top four in scoring.

HIGH SCHOOL

Before his freshman year, Zion and his parents decided that he would go to Spartanburg Day School. The tiny private high school was a unique choice for a star athlete. When Zion first decided to attend, they didn't even have a full-time basketball coach. Four years later, when Zion left high school, the Spartanburg Griffins had won three state championships in a row!

If you ask Zion about how going to a small private high school impacted him, he does not talk about **recruiting**. He is thoughtful and **introspective**. "I think it helped with my personality," Zion said. "It helped me bond with kids I probably wouldn't have bonded with…. It helped me become a more social person."

----

recruiting: when someone from a college invites a high school athlete to join their team

introspective: when one examines their own thoughts or feelings

The summer before Zion's freshman year of high school, his game began to transform. He grew 6 inches between 8th and 9th grade alone. He grew so fast, most of his clothes didn't fit him by the time he started as a freshman! In 9th grade, he was 6-foot-3. He averaged 24.4 points and 9.4 rebounds per game. And from 9th to 11th grade, Zion grew 3 more inches and put on about 75 pounds.

Over the course of those years, Zion transformed from an athletic point guard to a physically dominating power forward. The crowds at Griffin basketball games suddenly got bigger. Videos were posted to social media featuring a new Zion dunk nearly every day. One morning, the teenager woke up to more than 100 text messages. The night before, the famous musician Drake had posted a photo of himself wearing Zion's high school jersey!

Zion gets air while playing against the Boston College Eagles.

CHAPTER 4

Zion soars toward the hoop for a dunk during the 2018 McDonald's All American dunk contest.

TAKING OFF

Despite his athletic ability and high school stats, not everyone believed in Zion. Sure, they saw videos of his amazing dunks. But could a kid from a small town in South Carolina really play with the best athletes in the country? Was he ready for the big time?

Zion continued to set the basketball world on fire. He **dominated** the competition in South Carolina during his freshman and sophomore seasons. He also showcased his talents around the country. In June 2016, Zion was the leading scorer at the NBPA Top 100 camp. The next August, he won the Under Armour Elite dunk contest in New York.

----
dominate: to be much more successful than others in a game or competition

Zion wrecks the rim during the Chick-fil-A Classic in 2016.

His junior year, Zion's talent and notoriety increased even more. At the Chick-fil-A Classic tournament, Zion scored 53 points against highly recruited players. Suddenly, people started paying more attention to his near-40-points-per-game average. Zion was being talked about as one of the top-ranked high school basketball players in the US. During his junior season, Zion went on to receive about three dozen basketball scholarship offers. Louisiana State University even offered him a scholarship to play football!

Everyone around him was sure Zion would stay close to home. They expected him to attend South Carolina's Clemson University. But early in his senior season, Zion shocked friends and family. He decided to attend Duke University in North Carolina. In an ESPN interview, he explained his decision. "Duke stood out because the **brotherhood** represents a family. And Coach [Krzyzewski], he's just the most legendary coach to ever coach college basketball. I feel like, going to Duke University, I can learn a lot from him. . . . And like I said, the brotherhood—it just represents family, and I'm all about family."

---

brotherhood: a group of people who feel friendship, support, and understanding among themselves

Zion was excited to play for Coach K while at Duke University.

CHAPTER 5

DUKE

Zion began his career at Duke in 2018. He was part of the most talented recruiting class in NCAA history. Duke was able to grab the three top-rated high school basketball players in the country. The number-one ranked player was RJ Barrett. He had dominated at the McDonald's All American Game. He had also helped lead Canada to the gold medal at the FIBA Under-19 World Cup. But many scouts believed Cam Reddish was going to be the best player of the three. Zion was the biggest question mark. Would the kid from a small town in South Carolina make it? Questions remained about whether he could succeed against his tough competition.

After only a few games during his freshman college season, it was clear that Zion could play. He quickly showed that he was up to the challenge of playing with the pros. The entire basketball world became certain that Zion, not Barrett or Reddish, would be the overall number-one player drafted into the NBA. Duke's basketball coach, Mike "Coach K" Krzyzewski, calls Zion "the most unique athlete I've coached at Duke." He also thinks Zion the person is special. To ESPN, Coach K said, "There are sunshine people and cloudy people. He's brilliant sunshine."

Zion falls on the hardwood during a game against North Carolina, injuring his knee—and destroying his left shoe!

Zion did have one scare during his freshman season. He was playing against Duke's biggest rival, the University of North Carolina. Just 33 seconds into the game, Zion tried to plant his left foot. His size-14 Nike shoe ripped apart! Zion sprained his knee and missed the next few games. The next time Zion played, he was wearing custom Nike shoes. Reporters asked Zion many questions about the shoes after the game ended. "The shoes were incredible in this game," Zion said with a smile.

CHAPTER 6

Zion battles for the ball against the Spartans' Xavier Tillman, during the 2019 NCAA Men's Basketball Tournament.

DRAFTED

The Duke Blue Devils finished Zion's freshman season with a regular-season record of 26–5. They secured a number-one **seed** in the NCAA tournament. Although they easily made it through the first three rounds, they stumbled against a tough Michigan State team in the Elite Eight. Still, Zion had already proven his point. He was a star. The kid from Florence had the ability to play amongst pros.

A few months later, the New Orleans Pelicans shocked the world by winning the NBA draft lottery with only a 6.3 percent chance. Of course, the entire basketball universe knew exactly who the Pelicans would select on June 20, 2019: Zion Williamson.

----
seed: in sports, part of a bracket system that determines who will play whom in a competition

A few weeks before the draft, the Pelicans traded superstar Anthony Davis to the Los Angeles Lakers. They ended up getting an exciting group of talented young players. When draft night finally did arrive, the entire city of New Orleans was abuzz.

Meanwhile, in New York City, Zion was waiting for his name to be called. He didn't have to wait long. Commissioner Adam Silver approached the microphone. "With the first pick in the 2019 NBA draft, the New Orleans Pelicans select Zion Williamson, Duke University."

The crowd applauded. The city of New Orleans partied in the streets. As for Zion, he quickly wrapped his mother up in a hug. All of his hard work and **dedication** had paid off.

Zion was interviewed by ESPN's Maria Taylor a few moments later. She asked, "Is there anything that you'd like to say to your new team and family in New Orleans?"

Zion smiled from ear to ear. "Let's dance," he said.

---

dedication: a feeling of commitment or strong loyalty to something

Zion is congratulated by NBA Commissioner Adam Silver after being drafted by the New Orleans Pelicans.

CAREER HIGHLIGHTS

Zion Williamson's career is only just beginning, and it promises to be filled with excitement. But he's already come a long way. Here are some of the milestones along his journey so far.

Zion joins a local basketball team, the Sumter Falcons, at age 5. He plays and dominates against 9-year-olds.

 Zion's mother, Sharonda Sampson, coaches him on his middle school team. She is tough on him, and he later says she is the toughest coach he ever had.

Zion grows 6 inches during the summer before his freshman year at Spartanburg High School.

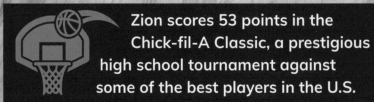 Zion scores 53 points in the Chick-fil-A Classic, a prestigious high school tournament against some of the best players in the U.S.

Zion wins his third straight state title, scoring 37 points with 17 rebounds and 6 blocks.

Zion plays in the McDonald's All American Game with two other Duke stars—RJ Barrett and Cam Reddish.

Zion plays his first game at Duke, against the University of Kentucky. He scores 28 points on just 13 shots.

Zion's Nike sneaker explodes as he tries to plant his left foot in a game against North Carolina.

Zion gets selected as the number-one overall pick in the 2019 NBA draft. In his post-draft interview, he says, "Let's dance!"

QUIZ

2 Who coached Zion's middle school basketball team?

1 Where did Zion Williamson grow up?

3 How many inches did Zion grow between 8th and 9th grade?

4 Which famous musician posted a photo of himself wearing Zion's high school jersey?

6 What team picked Zion in the 2019 NBA draft?

5 Zion accepted a scholarship to which university?

GLOSSARY

baseline: the line on a basketball court that is located behind the backboard at either end of the court

brotherhood: a group of people who feel friendship, support, and understanding among themselves

dedication: a feeling of commitment or strong loyalty to something

dominate: to be much more successful than others in a game or competition

draft: a system where professional sports teams choose players from high school or college

introspective: when one examines their own thoughts or feelings

jumper: an attempt to score a basket by jumping straight up in the air and shooting the ball while in the air

recruiting: when someone from a college invites a high school athlete to join their team

scholarship: money given to a student by a university to help pay for their education

seed: in sports, part of a bracket system that determines who will play whom in a competition

INDEX